HELLO, I'M TAI!

Koromon

Agumon

Greymon

...and these are my new Digimon friends! Wait until you hear how I met them.

ONE DAY AT SUMMER CAMP A WEIRD THING HAPPENED...

It started to snow
and we were somehow
transported to...

DIGIWORLD!!!

I didn't know where I was, or what this thing was in my hand!

I found out it was a Digivice.

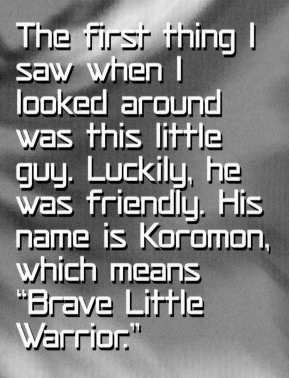

The first thing I saw when I looked around was this little guy. Luckily, he was friendly. His name is Koromon, which means "Brave Little Warrior."

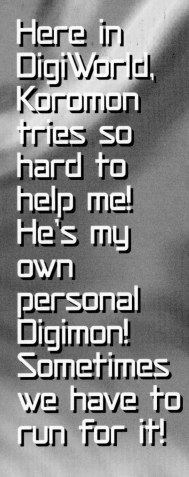

Here in DigiWorld, Koromon tries so hard to help me! He's my own personal Digimon! Sometimes we have to run for it!

MY HUMAN

Some of the other kids who went to camp with me ended up in DigiWorld, too. Here they are!

Matt
A good guy. He can be kind of stubborn, to say the least!

T.K.
Matt's little brother — really hangs in there.

FRIENDS:

Izzy
A computer genius! A useful guy to have around in DigiWorld.

Sora
Like a sister to me, she looks out for everybody!

Mimi
She's a trooper even if she would rather be at the mall!

Joe
Smart, but boy does he worry about everything!

THE GOOD

Motimon
Izzy's Digimon

Tsunomon
Matt's Digimon

Koromon
My Digimon

We found out that Digimons can be good — or bad. Here are some of the good ones that have become our own personal protectors!

Yokomon
Sora's Digimon

DIGIMONS:

Tokomon
T.K.'s Digimon

Bukamon
Joe's Digimon

Tanemon
Mimi's Digimon

We all seem to have a knack for trouble...

KOROMAN DIGIVOLVES!!!

You know what's cool about Digimons? They can Digivolve!

Through the mystical powers of our Digivices, when we need help or protection, they turn into strong warriors in the battle against evil! The first stage they Digivolve to is called "Rookie."

We couldn't believe our eyes when we saw our Digimons changing into Rookies to fight Kuwagamon, the giant beetle-like monster!

Meet my amazing Rookie Digimon, Agumon! He Digivolved from Koromon.

AGUMON HAS A SECRET WEAPON

"Pepper Breath!"

That fiery breath of my little guy gets 'em every time. Ouch!

He can even start campfires...

And thaw out frozen clothes!

MY DIGIVICE AND HOW

When I'm in trouble and Agumon needs to Digivolve, my Digivice kicks in!

It turns good Digimons into bigger, more powerful fighters, right when I need help most!

TO USE IT

The Digivice is an ancient, mystical weapon against evil.

Look how it helped save me from Leomon in a bad mood!

WHEN GOOD TURN

FEAR THE BLACK GEAR

Those evil Black Gears turn even the good guys bad. When that happens, look out!

Leomon
Once his Black Gear was out Leomon told us we were "Digidestined" to save the world!

DIGIMONS BAD

Frigimon

This giant snowman attacked me and Agumon in Freeze Land, but after we got his Black Gear out, he helped us find Matt.

Andromon

Andromon helped us escape from an old factory after we got the Black Gear out of his leg.

Meramon

A good Digimon who guards a volcano, he attacked us until we got his Black Gear out.

Monzaemon

This big teddy bear Digimon runs a happy Toy Town — until he gets a Black Gear in him!

When we get the Black Gears out, the bad Digimons turn good again.

Joe had quite a ride getting the gear out of Unimon!

Unimon

MY CREST: COURAGE

Gennai told us we each had a crest. When we found our crests, our Digimons could Digivolve to even higher levels.

Gennai

There are lots of different lands in DigiWorld, like File Island, Primary Village, and Infinity Mountain. I found my crest in a cave on the continent of Server!

BIGGEST AND EVER!

Kuwagamon had teeth like knives and scissor hands!

I thought Shellmon had me for sure!

BEST BATTLES

I thought we'd never get out of Etemon's Pyramid!

Greymon turned Shellmon into fish bait!

Greymon vs. Leomon!

Frigimon gets ugly.

Devimon blew us away but we got over it.

Monzaemon has a way of keeping you captive!

Everyone
attacked
Devimon
at once!

Metal
Greymon
BLASTS
Shogunmon.

Datamon sent all these little bad guys after us!

Even an avalanche can't stop Greymon.

We're sucked into the vortex!

WHAT'S COOL DIGIWORLD

You get to camp with friends.

We learn things from the good Digimons (minus their Black Gears)!

ABOUT

I love it when we find something to eat! (Even if it is just a bunch of eggs.)

A swim once in a while is cool.

Here's Piximon — isn't he, well, pixie-ish?

WHAT BUGS DIGIWORLD

There's NEVER enough to eat!

It's not real, it's digital! (Or is it???)

ME ABOUT

I can't stand
Gekomon or
Numemon (totally
hygiene deficient)!

Do you call this food?

Demidevimon is
a real pain.

JUST PLAIN THE MOST EVIL

Devimon, ruler of the evil Digimons!

BAD! PURELY DIGIMONS

Etemon

Myotismon

Devimon

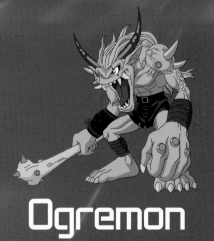

Ogremon

These guys don't EVER have a good side. They are just out to take over DigiWorld — AND the real world — and they don't care what they have to do to get their way!

MY BEST FRIENDS

Sora is, well... really okay. She might be a kid but she's pretty grown up, too. She gives me good advice (even if I don't always listen).

HUMAN

I like Matt but...

Matt and I don't always see eye to eye.

I think he's more sensitive than he lets on, but he sure does act like a tough guy. He drives me crazy sometimes!

ALL ABOUT

My best buddy!

My brave
friend vs.
Kuwagamon.

AGUMON

Agumon is always by my side... and the other Digimons love him too.

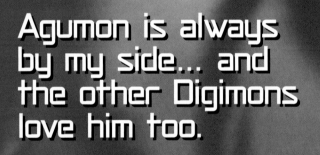

Uh-oh... is that Ogremon in the next stall?

Agumon and Palmon sneak into Myotismon's castle in disguise.

Piximon shows us how to Digivolve correctly!

To Digivolve, our Digimons have to be very well fed. As we learned from Piximon, they especially need to eat a lot to Digivolve past the Rookie level — to the Champions they are capable of being!

Here's Agumon stuffing in preparation for the next big Digivolve!

THE GREAT

When I'm in really big trouble and need extra big powers, Agumon Digivolves to the Champion level — GREYMON!

One of the first bad Digimons Greymon had to fight was an evil version of himself that Etemon sent to attack us!

GREYMON!

As Gennai had told us, in times of greatest danger, our Digimons can evolve even further to their Ultimate levels. They need the help of our crests to do this. Here my crest does its work and so does Greymon. He Digivolves into Metal Greymon!

NOVA BLAST!!!
Greymon's special weapon is a fire-blast more powerful than... well, anything!

Andromon is no match for Greymon and Garurumon!

After we got back to my real world through a digital dimensional warp, Greymon and I had to fight the evil Digimons that Myotismon sent to destroy the Earth!

CAN WE EVER TO EARTH?

Sora misses the smell of clean shirts.

Even though we get pulled back at times to fight, it sure would be nice to really go home for good.

I want to eat and take a bath.

GET BACK

I wonder how and what my parents are doing.

I miss my sister Kari.

I wish I could play soccer again.

THE ADVENTURE CONTINUES...

I know one thing for sure. There's a ton of excitement ahead for all of us!